AF270387

Great Chicago Fire

by Julie Murray

Dash!
LEVELED READERS
An Imprint of Abdo Zoom • abdobooks.com

Level 1 – Beginning
Short and simple sentences with familiar words or patterns for children who are beginning to understand how letters and sounds go together.

Level 2 – Emerging
Longer words and sentences with more complex language patterns for readers who are practicing common words and letter sounds.

Level 3 – Transitional
More developed language and vocabulary for readers who are becoming more independent.

abdobooks.com

Published by Abdo Zoom, a division of ABDO, PO Box 398166, Minneapolis, Minnesota 55439. Copyright © 2024 by Abdo Consulting Group, Inc. International copyrights reserved in all countries. No part of this book may be reproduced in any form without written permission from the publisher. Dash!™ is a trademark and logo of Abdo Zoom.

Printed in the United States of America, North Mankato, Minnesota.
052023
092023

Photo Credits: Alamy, Getty Images, Shutterstock
Production Contributors: Kenny Abdo, Jennie Forsberg, Grace Hansen, John Hansen
Design Contributors: Candice Keimig, Neil Klinepier

Library of Congress Control Number: 2022947151

Publisher's Cataloging in Publication Data

Names: Murray, Julie, author.
Title: Great Chicago fire / by Julie Murray
Description: Minneapolis, Minnesota : Abdo Zoom, 2024 | Series: Historical disasters | Includes online resources and index.
Identifiers: ISBN 9781098281236 (lib. bdg.) | ISBN 9781098281939 (ebook) | ISBN 9781098282288 (Read-to-me ebook)
Subjects: LCSH: Disasters--Juvenile literature. | History--Juvenile literature. | Great Fire, Chicago, Ill., 1871--Juvenile literature.
Classification: DDC 977.311--dc23

Table of Contents

Great Chicago Fire 4

Fire Factors 10

The Aftermath 16

More Facts 22

Glossary 23

Index 24

Online Resources 24

Great Chicago Fire

The Great Chicago Fire began on the night of October 8, 1871. The city of Chicago burned for more than 24 hours.

The fire began in the southwest side of the city in Patrick and Catherine O'Leary's barn. Most believe it started when a lantern was knocked over.

However, the exact cause of the
fire is still a mystery.

The fire spread rapidly. It burned through neighborhoods and the downtown **business district**. Firefighters spent hours battling the flames. Rain helped put out the fire on October 10.

DANGER

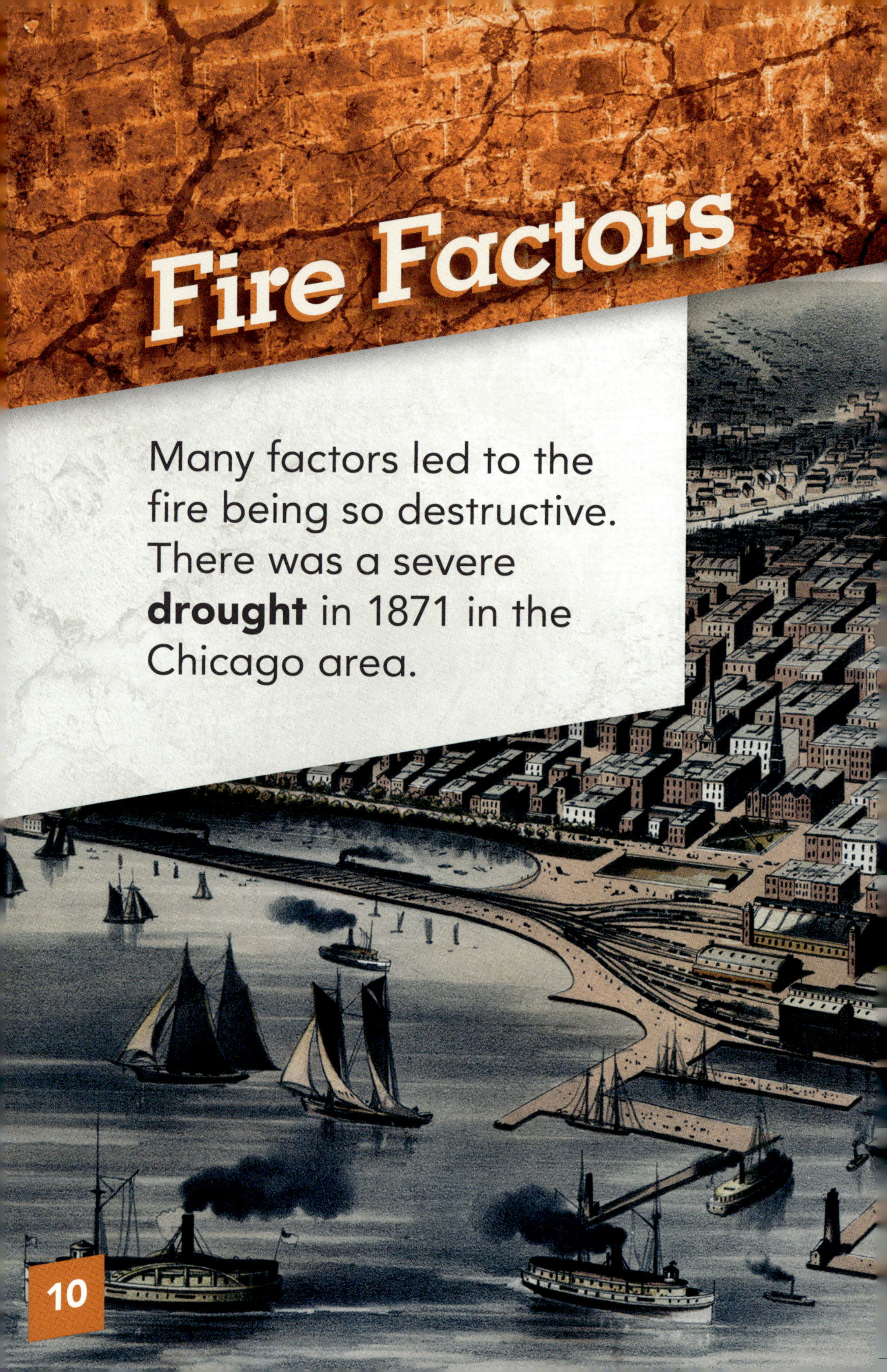

Fire Factors

Many factors led to the fire being so destructive. There was a severe **drought** in 1871 in the Chicago area.

No significant rain had fallen in more than three months. There were many hot, dry days leading up to the fire.

Most of Chicago's buildings were made of wood. This fueled the fire. The structures were also built close together. The fire jumped easily from one building to the next.

ODS

A cool, steady wind blew the fire north. The cool air created **fire whirls**, which sent the flames more than 100 feet (30 m) into the air!

15

The Aftermath

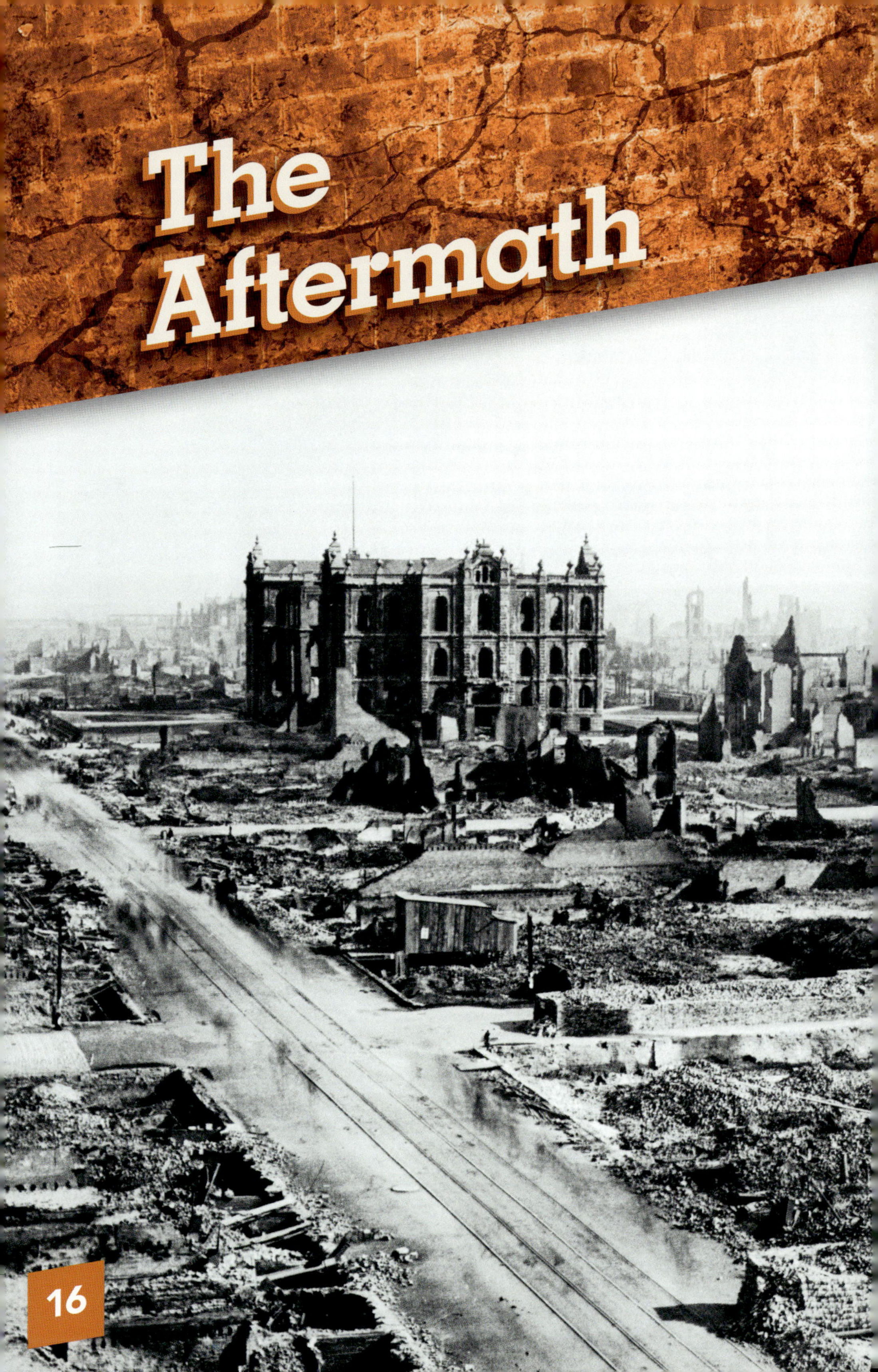

The fire destroyed 3.5 square miles (9 sq km) of Chicago. It burned more than 17,000 structures, including banks, hotels, railroad **depots**, and theaters.

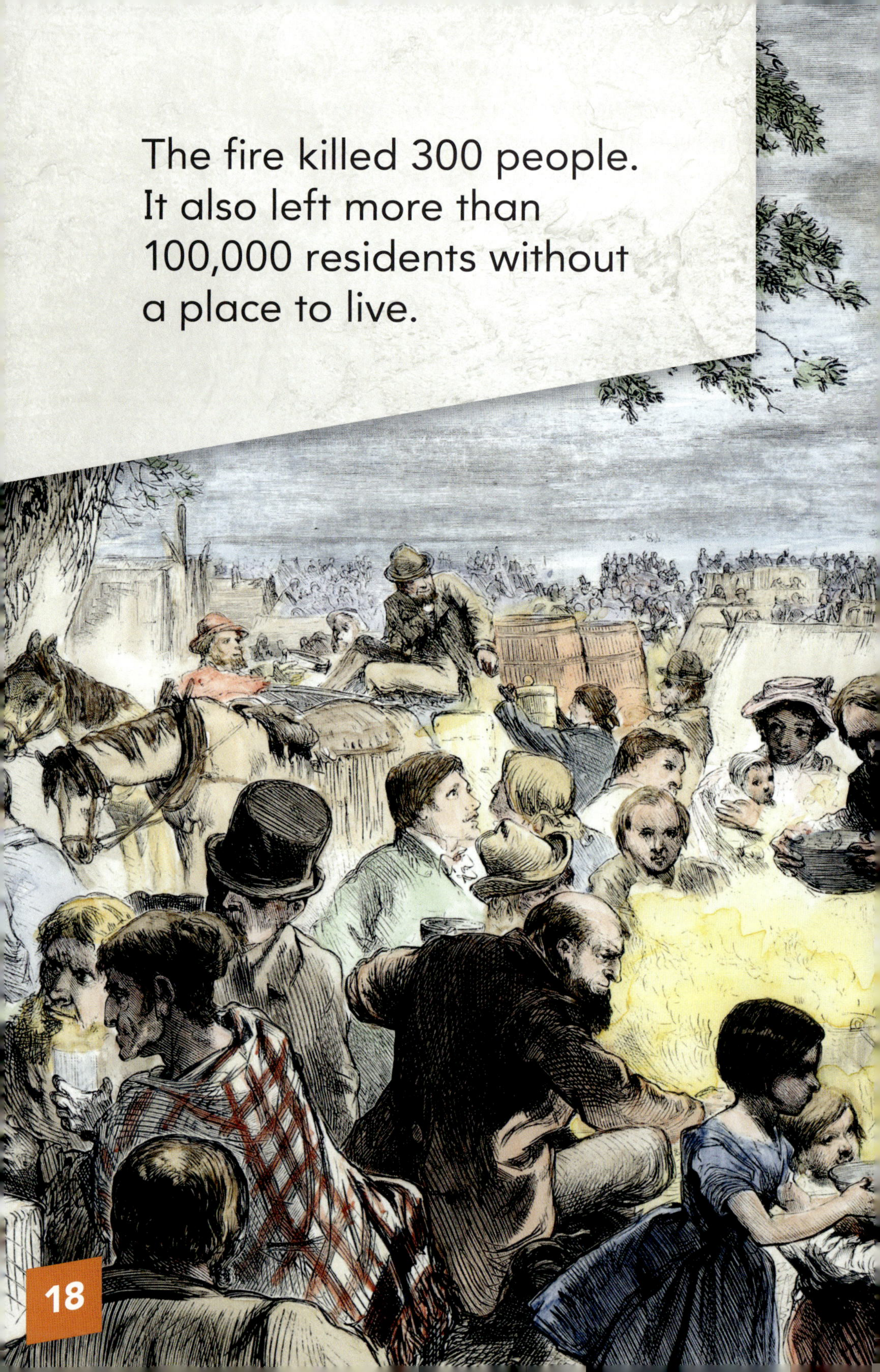
The fire killed 300 people. It also left more than 100,000 residents without a place to live.

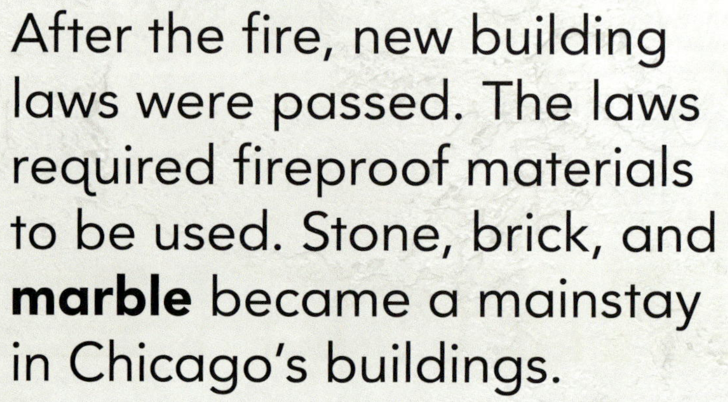

After the fire, new building laws were passed. The laws required fireproof materials to be used. Stone, brick, and **marble** became a mainstay in Chicago's buildings.

GIORGIO ARMANI
21

- The fire did $200 million in damage. Today, that would equal about $4.5 billion!

- The "Great Rebuilding" of Chicago began right away. The downtown was rebuilt within two years.

- The Chicago Fire Academy opened in 1961 on the site where the fire started. Today, it is called the Robert J. Quinn Fire Academy.

Glossary

business district – a part of a city or town where there are many businesses.

depot – a train station.

drought – a long period with little or no rain.

fire whirl – also known as a fire tornado or convection whirl, a large spinning flame that is created when very hot air comes into contact with cooler air.

marble – a kind of stone that can be cut and polished to be a hard, shiny surface.

Index

casualties 18

causes 6, 10, 11, 13, 15

Chicago, Illinois 4

damage 4, 8, 10, 13, 17

firefighters 8

O'Leary Farm 6

rebuilding 20

Online Resources

To learn more about the Great Chicago Fire, please visit **abdobooklinks.com** or scan this QR code. These links are routinely monitored and updated to provide the most current information available.